Praise

"I felt myself transcend while reading this. Emmett takes the struggle of the human experience and writes it into something beautiful. I'm still carrying the weight of this book with me. It meets you at your most honest, vulnerable self, gently takes your hand, and guides you home."
— Makenzie Campbell, author of *2am Thoughts*

"Audrey Emmett's *Don't Be a Stranger* is a striking collection that details a sincere exploration of love, heartbreak, and mental health. A brilliant mix of poetry and prose, Emmett's storytelling and imagery work as its own type of partnership throughout the book. Readers will undoubtedly feel seen reading this collection — anyone can find something valuable in *Don't Be a Stranger*."
— Ari B. Cofer, author of *paper girl and the knives that made her*

"If you've known heartbreak's dull ache, how it lingers in your bones and burrows into your heart, *Don't Be a Stranger* will feel like validation, a hug, and a punch in the gut all at once. Audrey Emmett's sophomore collection is deeply confessional, brutally honest. It's easy to fall into these pages and lose yourself in the narrative, which reminds us that trying to forget about those that have left us is not the same as actually forgetting them. Interspersed with artwork and handwritten pages that fans of Emmett's Instagram will adore, *Don't Be a Stranger* asks us to look in the mirror and forgive the person we became when we were hurting. It asks us to let it go."
— Caitlin Conlon, author of *The Surrender Theory*

"Audrey's newest collection proves herself as a profound writer. It is evident throughout the pages that she carefully placed these poems.

She wears her heart on her sleeve within this work. Her choice words, her stylish metaphors, and her bravery, are so poetically charged any reader will feel what she feels. This collection is meant to be absorbed and sat with. Soak in this lovely, fearless stack of vulnerability."

— Zane Frederick, author of *Itch*

"A singularly special anthology that exquisitely captures every morsel of Big Love — even the bits we'd prefer not to taste. *Don't Be a Stranger* is an ode to lust, love, and longing."

— Haley Jakobson, author of *Old Enough*

"*Don't Be a Stranger* is a hauntingly beautiful collection about heartbreak and surviving in the aftermath of loss. With poems and prose intermixed with Emmett's art that we know and love, this book will resonate with anyone who has experienced love and loss."

— Shelby Leigh, author of *changing with the tides*

"Equal parts brave and vulnerable, *Don't Be a Stranger* is a powerful collection of poetry navigating the all-encompassing nature of desire. Audrey Emmett invites you to love and to lose and to chase hope through the dark with her."

—Trista Mateer, author of *Honeybee*

"Audrey Emmett's sophomore poetry collection is a stunning tribute to love, heartbreak, and the things we do to endure both. Cathartic, powerful, and deeply moving, *Don't Be a Stranger* is for anyone who is dizzy with longing, anyone searching for a light in the dark, anyone who is ready to heal. Through her painfully honest poetry and prose, Emmett teaches us that it's okay to hold onto love — and helps us let go when it's time."

— Clara McGowan, author of *This Is All I Have to Give You*

Don't Be a Stranger   Audrey Emmett

Copyright © 2023 Audrey Emmett
Cover Design © 2023 Audrey Emmett
Cover Photo © Lauren Tepfer
Interior Design © 2023 Audrey Emmett
Interior Images © 2023 Audrey Emmett

Edited by Caitlin Conlon

All rights reserved. No part of this book may be used or reproduced in any manner whatsoever without written permission from the author except in the case of brief quotations embodied in critical articles and reviews.

This is a work of fiction. Names, characters, places, and incidents either are the product of the author's imagination or are used fictitiously and any resemblance to actual persons, living or dead, business establishments, events or locales is entirely coincidental.

DON'T BE A STRANGER

Paperback ISBN: 979-8-9867052-4-8
eBook ISBN: 979-8-9867052-1-7

For my mom

Content Warning:
This book contains poetry relating to topics that may be sensitive for certain readers, including: alcohol, blood (metaphorical, non-graphic), body image, mental health, and sex.

Anyway, don't be a stranger.
— PHOEBE BRIDGERS, "SCOTT STREET"

Brace for impact

I know, when you leave, I won't call you. Instead, I'll start watching planes in the sky. Instead, I'll watch shadows dance on the bottom of the pool. Instead, I'll watch myself start to slip away.

I know, when you leave, I'm going to listen to the songs that you showed me, rubbing salt in the wound. I'm going to walk around with a saw-toothed hole in my heart the size of your smile. And when you leave, I know I'll write about how I don't miss you, not at all. But I'll sink into bed at 3 in the afternoon and read the dictionary again. I still can't find the word that means wanting to live inside someone's eyes. The word that means wanting to bury love alive.

Life of crime

I dragged my eyes all over your face, like I was casing the joint. Like I was trying to memorize all of your features in case of a lucky break. Your eyes like dried fields, your mouth like a trap. I don't know if you noticed my tender trespass, but if you did, you didn't say anything. You just smiled, your lips twisted up like barbed wire.

And I thought, *This is what I've waited all day and night for.*

For your eyes to catch mine like a stolen key in a lock, for that crooked smile.
So I held on to that moment with a closed fist, wanting it to go unfinished for the rest of my life.

If this is it, I thought, *if this is my whole life,*

this is enough.

Transatlantic

The summer is punctuated by nights spent with his skin stuck to mine. Nights spent keeping ourselves floating on the surface of sleep.

"I have to go," I'm always saying, an hour past the time I told my mother I'd be home.

"Just ten more minutes," he whispers into my skin. And I give in. Of course, I give in.

I drive home at 2 a.m. in a moonstruck stupor. Two weeks later I take a transatlantic phone call in a coffee shop in Portland. He spends ten minutes lamenting my absence. I tell him I'll be worth the wait. A picture of me exists somewhere, taken on a disposable camera. A phone pressed to my ear, looking embarrassingly lovesick while I grin down at my lap.

I cannot keep track of my heart these days. It's always chasing after him, like a dog after a bone, shaking wet with want.

I miss him all the time. Sometimes I miss him when he's right in front of me. I think it might be anticipatory longing. Whenever the end of August enters my periphery vision, I put on my blinders.

Please, not yet.

Just ten more minutes.

Unfamiliarity

The freckles on your back remind me of a map I've not yet traced
of constellations undiscovered
You're made up of spindly limbs and pointed bones
cartilage here and there
but I can't see it
When I look at you
all I see is uncharted territory
When I look at you
all I see is something brand new

Put your dukes up

I'm unarmed
when longing corners me
while I'm driving home on a Tuesday night

Dusk covers my car silently
and the streetlights blink on
one by one

It hits me
like a blow to the chest
and I'm defenseless
against this desire

It knocks me out cold

Time moves faster than desire

I watch time pass by
let my eyes shift out of focus
let the colors bleed together
The summer painted by Monet

This longing aches
Of course it does

Not in the way it's supposed to
but in a way that calls me back
again and again and

I hope you never want something
the way that I want you

Eden

I'm in no hurry, baby
Take your time taking care of me
Low light, record player
My name on your lips like a sacred prayer

How sweet is it, really?
When you tell me I'm so pretty
Tangled hair, my red mouth
You go
south
south
south

Flushed apples of my cheeks, bite marks on my skin
The earliest snare, the original sin
Desire climbs my body like ivy
until finally
finally
we concede

Intime / Intimate

Run a finger down my spine,
crack me open,
and read me between the lines.
Pore over my pages, drinking in every word,
until your brow sweats and your vision blurs.
I'm built from ink and paper, but I'll unstitch you just the same.
Stroke me until I'm smudged,
breathe me in, say my name.

Getaway car

I enter every room with an escape plan
with every exit in my line of vision
You picked me up
took me by surprise
and I had no time to plan
how I'd quietly steal away
But three months later
you looked at me
your mouth on my navel
and I found I was so deep inside this house
there was no way to retrace my steps
No exits in sight
No escape hatch to climb through

But baby
I didn't need one
For you
I called off the getaway car
For you
I retired the disappearing act
You said *Stay awhile*
And for you
I did

Moving boxes

We finish making love on the duvet, strewn on the floor next to four moving boxes. Your room is empty, and the smell of sex still makes me blush. We sit side by side, our skin sticky and sweet. You press your lips to the caps of my shoulders and then to my throat. While I try to think of anything but the length of the distance that will soon separate us.

What a stupid thing, to be jealous of a toothbrush. Of a duvet cover.

It kills me, how much I want to be more than a memory you pack away, something you revisit when you pass through your hometown. It kills me, how much I want to be something you can't leave without.

i am yours
you are mine
you have my heart
you didn't even need a knife

I want to know you forever

The air was heavy between us. The alarm clock, glowing green in the darkness, spelled out 3:16 a.m. "Are you still awake?" he whispered.

"Yes," I mumbled, burying my head in his chest. "Are you?"

"Yes." I could hear the smile in his voice. A moment passed, but I don't think either of us noticed. "Can I ask you something?"

I reached up and touched his face. Traced a finger along his forehead, down the slope of his nose, over the outline of his lips. "What is it?"

He exhaled. In the dark, I could barely make out his silhouette. But I would recognize him anywhere.

He kissed me. An open-mouthed, fleeting kiss. "Do you think we'll still know each other when we're really old?" He said it quickly. "Like forty-five?"

I looked up at him, my heart constricting in my chest.

And my throat tightened as I thought of all the distance that would soon unravel us. All of the states, all of the miles. How I didn't know anything. How I was pretending like I did.

I kissed him, long and hard. Like I was already trying to make up for lost time. "I hope so," I whispered against his mouth. "I want that."

"Me too. I want to know you forever."

He reached toward me, held my fingers to his lips. I felt his breath brush across my knuckles. Our foreheads pressed against each other until droplets of sweat collected there.

He sighed again, and I could hear us both trying to swim backwards. Against time. Against inevitability. Against every responsibility waiting for us at the edge of August.

Even when I thought I knew the ending, it didn't matter. In that moment, he knew me. Differently than anyone ever had. All the good in me was his.

Maybe it always will be. Even when we're really old.

Like forty-five.

I loved you.

you know the rest

It's early

Sweet summer morning and we said goodbye. What overwhelmed me the most was how young I felt. Standing in the kitchen in my underwear and a soft lilac t-shirt, a fist to my eye in an attempt to dam the saltwater spilling over. How utterly childlike I felt, while you wiped away my tears with your thumbs.

In the milky morning light, I let you hold me.

You told me to look at you so I did. A quick, unmasked look. You kissed my forehead, told me you loved me, that it would all be okay. Then you walked away. And I couldn't stop it.

It's only 10 a.m.
and I have lost all sense of my adulthood.

I HAVE LOST ALL SENSE OF MY ADULTHOOD

More than

There are things about you
that I cannot explain
that I don't wish to explain
There were moments spent
with you
that cannot fit inside a poem

I refuse to taint something
so unfathomable
by putting it into words

We were together
That was enough

In which I almost regret you

Somewhere, there's a universe where you didn't get in the backseat of that car. Somewhere, there's a universe where you didn't rest your hand on my knee and look at me like I was something holy. Where I looked back at you and didn't feel faultlessly at home. Somewhere, there's a universe where you didn't knit our mouths together every chance you got. Where you didn't leave me with a mouth full of yarn.

Somewhere, in a universe far, far away, we're waking up to each other on a Thursday morning. Succulents on the windowsill. An ambulance wailing in the distance.

Leave the light on

I'm still chasing hope
through the dark
like a lost dog

Graceless

I still remember it, you know. I remember the way your heart melted in my hands, in my mouth, dribbled down my chin. I remember the way you held my head against your chest and the way I cried. Ugly, heaving sobs that tore open the silence and left jagged scars in their wake. I remember the way we said goodbye. Wordless, just your breath in my mouth, just your forehead against mine. Just the closeness that comes before everything falls away.

I remember every part of it. Every part of you.

You're still gone, but I don't want to leave yet.

I'M HAVING A HELL OF A TIME, BURNING THROUGH MEMORIES TILL I'M IN THE RED

In every dream it's july

In every dream, it's like before
and you're walking through my front door.

Like a native, you say,
I've been trying to go home.

In every dream, I kiss you and say,
You are.

Meli's

I stretch my arms across the booth to where you sit, your hair mussed and your scruff grown out. It doesn't take much to unstitch me anymore. Just your green and golden eyes on mine. Just the trace of a smile playing on your lips. Just your fingertips drumming on the table. Our knees knock against each other. First accidentally, then on purpose. You grin at me and for a moment I forget where we are.

In a full room, you're the only one I see.
And in a full room, I come apart at the seams.

And it's not quiet. But we don't need to say anything.

State street

Orange light poured into the backseat of the cab until it was filled to the brim. I looked out my window and saw the pavement slick with rain, reflecting green then yellow then red then green. The driver was playing the kind of music that you can almost place. Just familiar enough to create a sense of weary nostalgia.

It was well past midnight as we moved slowly through traffic. I could feel the warmth of your gaze and I let it linger. I let you look at me, my face smeared with rain and laughter and light. After a few moments I turned toward you. And you looked back unabashedly, with dark eyes that I had never seen sharp nor vacant. Only soft. Always soft.

You reached up and cupped my face with your hand, still cold from the October rain. I leaned my cheek into it, turned my mouth and kissed the heel of your palm. You suddenly looked pained and I didn't have to ask why. I didn't have to say anything. In the back of that cab, we knew what it meant.

Easy like

He's standing in the kitchen in that T-shirt I like to wrap my fists around. "Scrambled, right?" he asks, glancing over his shoulder as he reaches for the pepper.

"Right," I nod, as I fill up the tea kettle with water from the sink. Normally I'm vehemently opposed to the tap, but he swears by the water from this side of the bay.

In the morning, the light refracts all over his kitchen, little bits of gold stippled across the countertop. It's nearly January, but we've opened all the windows and doors to the balcony and I can see the water from where I'm standing. Just a fraction of blue, glinting on the horizon.

I pour hot water into my mug and watch the tea bloom. Part of me feels like I'm trying to commit this all to memory, but I can't put my finger on why. I inhale, breathing in the scent of pine wafting in from the open windows and olive oil sizzling on the pan. The smell of this place, littered with memories: his voice, pouring all over me, all over the floor, making a mess of things. *God, if this is clutter then I can't stand to go without.*

We're moving slowly, to the silvery voice of some jazz singer floating across the morning air. He grabs the plates and we sit down close to each other at the kitchen table, where playing cards are still scattered from the night before. He reaches around my head, pulls out the tie from my hair. My curls spill over my shoulders, a stray strand falling into my eyes.

"Better," he hums, tucking into his eggs.

Sometimes it's hard to look at him, like he's the sun or something. I think of the pale light in his bed, his mouth flickering on my pulse, how his hands held me while I was falling apart. I sink in the memory, just a little, my cheeks flushed.

When we're finished we wash the dishes in the sink, soapy water up to our forearms. The wind picks up a little and I shiver. The air vibrates with the promise of a storm.

"I'd better go before I get caught in the rain," I say, walking barefoot across the tiled floor. The last ray of sun hits his face before being swallowed up by clouds.

In the foyer, we get caught up saying goodbye. Each thread of conversation we tug seems to unravel into something else, and before we know it, we're huddling on the porch while the clouds burst into a downpour.

"Just stay," he grins. "Or just tell me one more thing before you leave.

Just tell me everything."

Twain harte

It's January and we are eating dinner on the floor. I smile at you and you kiss pasta sauce from my chin. We drink old vodka from your parents' liquor cabinet and my chest is light, like I could float. It's January and we are drunk and you are getting higher, blowing smoke out of the window in the kitchen. I kiss your mouth and taste ash. I hardly mind as my teeth get numb. It's January and we pile blankets on the floor and build a fort out of rainbow sheets. The temperature drops. We play gin rummy and you let me beat you every time. It's January and we make pinky promises until we fall asleep. Two days later we'll get into our first fight and I'll cry, but you'll kiss my knees and my fingers and we'll make love against the shower door. It's January. It's January and I'm burning softly, quietly, with love. It's January. It's only just beginning.

They say you'll know when you've gone too far

Like they're giving directions / Like I'm crossing state lines / Like I'll know when I've reached the threshold / of where I end / and you begin / Like I'd know not to cross it / Like I wouldn't cross it just the same

Burnt offering

I don't know how to need something
without sacrificing myself for it

Three intimacies

1. You, wetting the pad of your thumb against your tongue to wipe away a stray lick of food from the corner of my mouth. My mouth is always dirty. Somehow you always come away clean.

2. A morning in Chicago, mid-February. A gray hotel room. Your hands brushing across my hair, my face. I don't remember much else.

3. When you washed my face the night we got drunk off tequila. We stood in the dimly lit shower, warm water running small streams down our skin, kissing until we were dizzy. Until the alcohol made our heads too fuzzy to stand. You washed my cheeks and I let you. You told me you loved me for the third time. Nothing has ever felt like that since then.

Cloak-and-dagger

You're still shaped like a question mark in every word I write about you. You sleep with secrets to keep you warm. This is all I know. This, and your breath on my cheek.

Do I really need to know the rest?

Emptying the moon

He traces the curve of my jaw like it's the outline of a waning moon. And out of the moon, from my jaw, blooms a desire so ardent I lose all sense of significance.

I sigh his name like a hymn. I swear the green of his eyes turns me holy halfway to hell. Down to my core, there's nothing more.

I don't know where the night began, but I know it will end with this: where the pale light of 2 a.m. is reflected.

In the backseat of my car, I feel my heart clawing and scratching its way out of my rib cage. At the bottom of the street, my body wanes beneath his touch. I'm running out of skin. And we are running out of moonlight. Slipping through our fingers, as the dawn spreads itself across the sky.

The faint glow of his skin evaporates as I turn the night over in my mind. And when the sun's rays grab hold of our flesh, he opens the car door with his foot. My eyes are still closed, but I can sense the vacancy where something breathing used to live. It isn't the first time.

The receding moon dangles above us, pallid and ashen.
An omen of everything still left to wane.

let my stomach
ache for months

TOTAL

just to feed you
adoration

Side effects might include: fatigue

You told me not to leave if I was too tired. But I insisted, and drove home in the rain, desperately trying not to fall asleep at the wheel. The windows greeted me darkly as I pulled into my driveway. But, like most nights I left your arms, I sat in the idling car for a few moments, my heart struggling to catch its breath.

(*You told me not to leave if I was too tired,*

Sheets of rain swept over the windshield as I let love's exhaustion engulf me. I almost let it swallow me whole. Until I caught my reflection in the rearview mirror, eyes filled with tired desperation, and I swung open the car door.

I knew if I'd sat there even a millisecond longer
I would've drowned in the realization.

but I was far too exhausted to stay.)

That love wasn't supposed to wear me out like this. My intestines weren't meant to knit themselves in knots, my heart wasn't meant to run itself weary. I wasn't meant to be loved in question marks.

The words *I love you* were never meant to feel like a relief,
rather than a given.

Misery is the thing with feathers

We laid side by side, the backs of our arms scarcely touching. His breath, slow and heavy, echoed against the unbearable silence.

My eyes, wide and unblinking, traced the hotel ceiling. I tried to make out shapes in the plaster, but my mind kept its habit of wandering back toward him. I tried to find it within myself to say something, but every time my mouth opened, my throat ached with the threat of tears. A sharp pain behind my eyes had begun to unfurl, like a web of cracks in a pane of glass.

Minutes ticked by. It was 3:58 a.m. And I laid awake, afraid of everything between us that we couldn't see.

Six hours ago, I stood in that 7-Eleven and caught a glimpse of myself in the security monitor. Under harsh fluorescent light, my skirt suddenly looked far too short. I tugged it down, ignoring the nagging in my stomach.

I'd never been good at naming my feelings. But if I was a cartoon character, the word *miserable* would've been circling my head like a halo of birds after a sharp blow to the skull.

His breath remained steady. I thought of earlier in the night, his cool detachment, how it came and went, how I'd almost come to crave it. The lows making the highs that much sweeter.

My hand twitched, and our fingers brushed against each other. I heard a sharp intake of breath.

My name left his lips, shaped like a question. I kept quiet.

"It's okay if you're still mad," he whispered, his voice unreadable.

The ceiling seemed soft, close to caving in. I knew I was too.

"I know," I murmured. I turned my head toward him, running my eyes along the profile of his face. Shadows danced over his troubled silhouette. Forgiveness plucked at my heartstrings.

"Let's just forget about it, okay?" And with that, I tried to replace the uncertainty swarming my brain with something else. I clung to the memory of us at the planetarium, laughing so hard that we had to gulp for air between fits of hysterics.

I could put a lid on my needs. This boy loved me. Isn't that all I could ever ask for? How dare I want more?

So, I ignored the birds circling. Despite their burgeoning resemblance to vultures.

In the dark, something hungry touched down between us. Something we couldn't see. But we both knew it was there.

If you ignore it for long enough

Maybe I am far too good
at leaving well enough alone

Valentine's day

A candy heart
melts away on my tongue
I'm yours

I swallow
and it burns
all the way down

Flowers in a styrofoam cup

I stepped out of the shower, droplets of water clinging to my skin. Wrapping a towel around my body, I stood in front of the mirror before dragging my fingers across its surface, wiping away the steam.

I studied my reflection. And my bare, wet, newly-nineteen-year-old face blinked widely back at me. I pretended not to notice how unfamiliar I looked, reasoning that it was probably the fact that I was a day older that made my own face so unrecognizable.

I shook my head as the mirror fogged up again, clouding the strange image from my eyes. I ran my fingers through my curls hurriedly as I heard him step through the hotel room, the door slamming shut behind him.

"Happy birthday!" he called from outside the bathroom door.

"Thanks," I smiled, stepping out into the bedroom.

My back was still wet when he handed me the supermarket daisies. His eyes met mine. "I got you flowers," he said, his voice tinged with annoyance. I knew what he meant.

This is what you wanted, right?

I pretended not to notice the way he looked at me. The way his voice bled all over the flowers, their petals flushed with disappointment.

A yellow price tag dangled from the stem.

I looked up at him. "Thank you." I stood on my tiptoes to kiss him quickly, then turned away before he could see the blush blooming in my cheeks.

I stood in the middle of the gray hotel room, clutching the towel to my body with one hand and the bouquet in the other, humiliation creeping its way up my neck.

"I don't think we have a vase." My voice sounded distant, and unfamiliar. It hung in the air.

I set the bouquet down on the desk and padded across the carpet toward the bathroom. As I filled a Styrofoam coffee cup with water from the tap, I caught another glimpse of myself in the mirror. It was like looking at someone else entirely.

Gingerly, I placed the bouquet inside the undersized cup. It teetered, threatening to spill all over the floor. But I pretended that it fit.

I pretended that this is what I wanted.

I looked toward him, his silhouette backlit against the frosted window.

I pretended I couldn't see what this had become.

Film

Sick to my stomach,
as I watch the credits roll.
In an empty theater, save for me.
A fool with the best seat in the house.

This is the end

You hold your hand out to help me from the backseat and I smile at you because you know I don't need it. It's a gesture. I know you're still laden with guilt. And a memory of this morning pierces me, suddenly. Of my mouth open against your chest. Of my tears smearing hot against your skin. I let go of your hand. The February air is bitter and I steel myself against it. Against you.

I watch you load my luggage into the second cab. I recognize you in a way I don't think will ever go away. But this morning, with the curtains closed, you were a stranger. I couldn't place your face for the life of me. For the life we'd built.

For the past eight nights, we'd fallen asleep holding each other. And for the past eight mornings, we'd awoken to something neither of us could have imagined. The best thing I never saw coming.

You push my glasses up the bridge of my nose and I flinch at the intimacy. It's hard to ignore. The morning like a shadow, like a stain, like a bruise. I keep pressing it to see if it still hurts.

Of course it does. You kiss me goodbye.

Of course it does.

you kiss me awake &
 I bite back my devotion

i can't bear to watch
you sacrifice it on
the altar of your ego

Acts of desperation

Sometimes it feels like I'm holding onto you for dear life. That's not how it should be, should it? Gulping down promises and stealing kisses, trying to memorize every freckle on your face in the fleeting light?

You kiss me awake and I bite back my devotion.
I can't bear to watch you sacrifice it on the altar of your ego.

Your promises of a shitty apartment in the hills, of sunset dog walks, of a life where distance doesn't make a fool of us both. All of it looks so frail in the daylight.

Your shadow crosses my doorway, and I start searching for synchronicities like my life depends on it.
Some sort of sign to prove me wrong.
Petals litter the floor
by the time you decide I'm worth making time for.
I don't have the dignity to tell you it was *He loves me not.*
I already knew the answer before I asked the question.

I don't know if I love you anymore, either. Love doesn't feel like gasping for air, does it? Love isn't slipping my key in your pocket when you aren't looking, only to find it resting on my kitchen counter the next day. Like a broken promise. Like an answered question.

Love doesn't live here. Neither do you.

Insatiable

If you wanted less love
why did you take it?

Naiveté

You promised you'd come home for me.
You came home, sure,
but it wasn't for me.

And I missed you
down to my bones,
down to my marrow.

I was so young.
I didn't know how to find myself in all that longing.

Run it dry

There isn't much to say. Or maybe there is, and we just aren't saying it. There's silence swimming between us, but neither one of us wants to drain it. Not yet. Because once it's gone, that's it. There will be nothing left between us. There's no love left, there are no goodbyes left. There's nothing left. And we'll have to walk away without ever knowing why or when or how this could have worked. So we'll swim in this silence until we don't. We'll drown in it if we have to.

There isn't much to say. But there is.
I just don't want to be the one to say it.

These are the things we don't talk about
(after Caitlin Conlon)

Your hand on my knee / The nights you spent holding me / How I couldn't ever really fall asleep / My voice crumpling over the phone / How the distance got wider / in more ways than one / That morning in February / when everything faded to gray / How every time I left / I wanted you to ask me to stay / The panic curling in my stomach / My tears smeared across your chest / All because you wouldn't let me love you / the way I wanted to / Those three days at my house / amidst the apocalypse / The amount of times / you changed your goddamn mind / Your voice over the phone / telling me you had nothing left to say / How you told me not to walk away / How you were the one that walked away

Bullseye, baby!

I think I always knew I was a shot in the dark.
But I still pressed my back
against the target,
still held my breath
while you took aim.
Still pitch-black-prayed you would hit your mark.

We both knew I wasn't dodging any bullets.
Why do you think I painted the bullseye
right over my heart?

Slapstick

It strikes me as funny, when my mother opens the garage door and lets me fall into her arms. I grin and bear it while I'm choking on the guilt that's been stuffed down my throat. I tell my therapist that it's hard to remember that my feelings matter. And I smile when she says, "Let's talk next week." I drive home on Friday night, and my defrosters won't work. I listen to songs about love so sincere it breaks your bones and I laugh till my lungs ache.

I am so numb.
I am so numb.

I am so goddamn numb.

Sleepovers in cemeteries

I sleep in a graveyard every night, where the sheets are haunted by ghosts of our past. The first time you possessed me, called me yours. And I wasn't even scared. At least, not like I used to be.

Our last night in August, when we weren't nearing extinction.
Our last night in March, when we were.

You broke me so many times between these sheets. The last time I heard your voice was in this bed: alone, crackling over the phone. Killing me slowly with every drawn-out sigh. Reducing me to an inconvenience. Just another exorcism to cross off your to-do list.

I hear every beginning and ending collide when my head hits the pillow. Each night, as sleep pulls me under, I clasp my hands against my lips, whispering ragged prayers into them.

Please let this all have been an unholy dream.
 Let me wake up to you talking in your sleep, thumbing my hip bones, your mouth hot against the nape of my neck.

Every morning, a cemetery for miles.

I THINK I TURNED EVERY PIECE OF YOU INTO SOME SORT OF RELIC

Foxhole

At least I can say this now without fear of losing something I never really had. I loved you.

Having said that, I think we can both agree that you saw a loose thread of longing and you pulled it. Until I came apart at the seams.

Maybe you couldn't help it. Which is to say you had never experienced love on all fronts before. But I can't compare this to a war. This was never a battle.

How could it be?

I laid down all my weaponry the first time you said my name.

Closing night

We didn't deserve to burn out the way we did. We deserved slamming doors and snide remarks and screaming. God, we deserved to scream at each other. We didn't deserve all this swallowed resentment, all this careful avoidance. Our ending warranted something just as fervent as our beginning. But you called me up at 8 p.m. and shut us down the way you shut down a carnival ride. Bright, spinning, beautiful,

then nothing.

Back to you

Every thought I have leads me back to you.
Sometimes I have to remind myself of your voice.
Other times
I can't stand how much of you I remember.

There are no right words to talk about this. Only wrong ones.
I'll say them anyway:
I still love you like nothing else.
In another life
we could've made it.
In this one you gave me up.
Maybe that's not true.
Or maybe it is.
Either way,
I guess that's everything.

Open season

It's been about a week since you took my heart in your mouth, chewed it up, and spit it out. And I keep forgetting to cry. Because every time I think of you and your mouth and my bloody pulp of a heart, the space behind my eyes goes numb.

I go running, a hollow attempt to outpace the sorrow that I know is hunting me down, snarling. And in hindsight, I guess my real mistake is hitting shuffle. Because three notes into that song and I'm stopped dead in my tracks. And then I'm not.

Because I'm spitting and crying and clawing at my own heart, trying to get this traitorous thing out of my chest. And nothing about this is beautiful. Not in the way they portray heartbreak in movies, bathed in blue and romantic in its own sense. This is ugly. It has teeth. And I'm a sitting target, standing in the middle of the street at one in the afternoon. Sweaty and sobbing.

And I am almost home. But I am nowhere near it.

Head-on

I wanted to wrap myself around you
like a car around a tree
Which is to say
nothing about us was worth saving
We were always fated to crash and burn

I miss you, I hope you're alright

I miss you a lot. I still remember everything
and lately I can't decide if I'd rather forget.
Every memory is still a breath away.
My nose pressed against your shoulder blade,
my lips tracing your freckles.
I still remember you as you were,
your eyes warm and your mouth open.
How you looked at me that night and told me not to go.
How can I possibly
come back from that?
I still know your birthday and your favorite song
and how your voice sounds when you love someone.
I still know everything that keeps you up at night.
Sometimes I am right back in that night in August,
when you asked if you could know me forever.
When I promised that you would.
Admittedly,
I still remember what it felt like to love you.
Like I had to apologize for it.
It's like this: maybe one day we'll be perfect for each other.
Or maybe one day I'll see you
and the part of me that still waits for you will die away.
Either way, I still wonder if you're doing alright.
I still hope you're doing alright.

Closer than never

Pulled myself apart just to earn your affection
In tatters just to hear you say you miss me

I just miss who I used to be

i'm scared love is
only worth something
to me
when it is just
out of reach

xoxo

i spent way too long trying to make something beautiful

EMMETT/AUDREYANNE
TSA PRE
SAN JOSE TO CHICAGO

UA2129
SJC-ORD GATE 15 BOARDING BEGINS: 6:20A SEAT 21A
THU OCTOBER 24 2019 GATE MAY CHANGE BOARDING ENDS: 6:45 AM WINDOW
FLIGHT DEPARTS: 7:00 AM ECONOMY
FLIGHT ARRIVES: 1:16 PM EXIT ROW

out of this

Linguistics
(after Caitlin Conlon)

In a language that doesn't have the word 'love' I say, "I still have all of the boarding passes from the flights I took to see you." I say, "sometimes just the thought of your knees brings me to mine." I say, "I wore the shirt you gave me to bed last week." I say, "it still smelled like when you'd get high," I say, "and I didn't even mind." I say, "I used to be stronger than this, didn't I?" I say, "but I can't stop thinking about all the dead languages," I say, "now we can add ours to the list."

I say, "just tell me I meant something to you." I say, "I don't even care if it's true." I say, "I'd still rather have you than any second-rate substitute."

I say, "it's been almost two months and I still miss hearing you say my name in your sleep." I say, "do you still say my name in your sleep?" I say, "I can't listen to 'Adeline' without folding in half." I say, "I'd live my life haunted by you if it meant you did too." I say, "maybe I should have said this earlier, " I say, "but I almost believed you when you said forever."

I say, "I know your fascination ran out once you saw me weak," I say, "but I still gave you everything." I say, "maybe that was wrong of me,"

I say, "but I forgot how to be anyone but yours."

I say, "let's do this again when we can get it right."
I say, "do you think we'll ever get this right?"

Playing with matches

Foolish
to believe
you could light me up
without burning me down

Break it, burn it, kiss it better

My hands are sticky with memories and I'm sick of getting stuck on every reminder of your tenderness. Not when it came at such a sore cost.

I lick my fingers and taste remembrance: when you wrapped me up and whispered promises in my hair. When I slurred *mine* against your lips, and you made a mess of me between my hips.

I am always forgetting the part where you split me open, gutted me like an animal you were getting ready to devour.

But I'm nineteen and all I know is mercy. All I know is exoneration. You ask for my forgiveness without realizing that it's already yours. It's always been yours.

Even before the thought of wreckage ever crossed your mind.

Snogging with sorrow

Even when I smile
grief is kissing my teeth

Brutal

God, isn't it tragic?
The way we burnt out
like a licked finger to a match
Burning bright then up in smoke

God, isn't it brutal?
The thought that maybe
we were nothing special
The thought that maybe
you packing your bags
and forgetting to turn off the lights
was nothing cataclysmic
but just another Tuesday
I'll be writing about
for the rest of my goddamn life

God, isn't it severe?
This is the end
and no one saw it coming
The plot twists
the knife
and I forget that I'm bleeding
until a stranger points it out
in the grocery line

Entrails

I'm trying to come to terms with all the ways
you still exist inside of me

The peach and the pit

I have memories
that are soft,
like overripe fruit.
They ooze and drip
when I touch them
(*sidewalk fireworks under a violet sky,*
sneaking out for night swims,
hazy, blissful mornings spent in a world of our own).
I'm always afraid they'll bruise,
and I can't bear to mar them
with my grieving touch.

And I have memories
you could chip a tooth on
(*that gray, unfocused morning in chicago,*
the phone call I took outside.
the night I wept on the bathroom floor,
then wiped my cheeks—
you could never tell when I wasn't fine).

These I don't mind crushing up,
turning to dust.
Blowing away.
Every time you broke my heart,
dispelling into
nothingness.

19

It's easier to call you a mistake
than something I'm still wiping from my mouth

More callous than casual

I wish I knew you for something else other than someone who broke my heart once. Or someone I thought of while I punished myself. I can't smell sunscreen without thinking of you, stretched out beside me on that boat. This makes me resent you and I wish it didn't. I wish I knew you as a stranger who smiled at me on the street once, or someone who always lent me a pen in class. I wish I never knew how your hair looked wet, or how that mole on your arm is shaped like a heart. You fucked me up. I kept thinking I knew you. Maybe I never really did.

Little fires all the way home

I drive around and feel bitter memories bubble up in my throat like bile. I swallow them back down. And sometimes it's easy—to swallow sitting in your passenger seat, smoke passing clean through me as someone sets the forest on fire. You tell me it's a controlled burn. I ask how you can control how much you hurt something.

Bruised

I want to put this down and walk away from it. But then I think of the nape of your neck and my heart rolls over in my chest. Every time I remember how my fingers would skip over the hollowness between your bones, my stomach halts and I hit the brakes. Sometimes I even have to pull over.

Yesterday, it was pouring rain and the clouds were the color of your skin after I bit it. I cut the defroster and let the windshield fog up with everything I could remember. And with my finger, I made a list on the window of all the ways I could love you better this time. All the ways I could erase the past and replace it with something as tender as the nape of your neck.

In which we don't dance around it:
a conversation

YOU: Maybe we ruined this by letting it sit out too long
ME: Like milk on the counter
YOU: Like fruit in the sun
ME: Are you saying this is rotten now?
YOU: Not rancid but
YOU: I wouldn't eat it
ME: Did you ever consider me, even for a moment?
YOU: For a moment, yes
ME: How long did it last?
YOU: Too long
ME: Then what would you call this?
YOU: A eulogy, maybe?
ME: A funeral seems long overdue for something as rotten as me and you

Fallacy

You went straight through me.
Like a knife,
like a dream.
Like something,
like nothing.
It all felt real to me.

AUTHOR	
TITLE	
DATE DUE	BORROWER'S NAME

YOU WERE THE
ONLY ONE
I'VE EVER WANTED
TO BELONG TO

Sunburnt

I sit here with sunburnt shoulders, my heart rattling in my chest. I'm not sure anymore if I miss you or if it's simply a habit I can't seem to break. But last night, I sat at the kitchen counter with my head in my hands, and I listened to each one of your voicemails. I heard your voice, torn up by static and distance and time, and tried to remember the shape of your mouth.

If you were here, you'd kiss the redness off my shoulders and I'd try my hardest not to cry. I know you always hated when I did. But, truthfully, you're the only one who brought it out of me.

Like skin to sun, I always turned tender for you.

Anti-love-letters

You never gave me any closure and I never asked for any.
But this feels like stitching something closed without any string.
These poems are just needles threading in and out of my skin.
And I'm bleeding all over the page,
just praying the blood dries pretty.

all the shitty things you said, i kept them

but that's besides the point

Call it even

Maybe I just don't want to admit
that I got the better end of it
All along I could sense your leaving
but I'd kill to know how you're feeling

I've been driving circles in my car
never make it very far
Still stuck in that night
when you couldn't give me a reason
Think I'm finally ready to call it even

I could've lived my entire life
trying to get it right
Where did you leave your decency?
Never thought you'd give up so easily

Your mouth against mine
we reached the end of the line
I was never going to make it out of this clean
But despite it all

I could've sworn we were evergreen

On the turn

I can live with knowing we loved each other
even if it wasn't for the long haul

i want to apologize to every person i haunted
while i was trying to avoid your ghost

This is the third to last one

I still think about him. Not when I'm with you, but I do. I think about him when my pen dips down onto paper. It still has so much to say about the way he ran away. I can't make sense of it, and maybe I never will. But I can't stop writing about the way he acted like loving me was a chore. Like mowing the lawn, like laundry on a Saturday afternoon. And maybe it's just July that's stirring up all of this fucking nostalgia, but I could say the same thing about February, November, and May.

Maybe I lost something in his hands. Maybe he's still holding it. And where's the closure in that? Where's the closure in any of this?

Some nights I swear I'm down on my knees, asking god when I'll finally run out of poems in which I depict the exact way he turned my heart inside out.

This is the last one, I swear.
This is the second to last one, I swear.

Every shade of green

I am envious of every past version of myself
how oblivious I was to your existence

Epithet

How could I call it love
when you couldn't call me anything at all?
All those times you said my name
(sharp around the edges
but out of focus just the same)
I misheard you
I thought you said baby
I thought you said honey
I thought you said you loved me
But you didn't
not at all
All those times
my name caught in your jaw
But you couldn't call me
anything
anything at all

Bloodstained

I don't know how to stop talking about the way you ripped me open
I need to stop calling attention to all my open wounds
but you had your gunshot hands all over me
the morning before you left

Maybe it's my fault
for digging up our grave
with my pen
over and over again

I'm just trying to figure out why this silence is so violent
and I'm tired of waking up in bed alone

I walk barefoot across my front lawn
bloody footprints in my wake
I keep trying to stitch myself back up
with strangers' hands
but I can't stand to be kissed
by any mouth but yours

Just give me an apology
and I'll never ask for more
Just make it up to me
and I'll leave my resentment
at the door

I'm still searching for somewhere to place the blame
because I can't bear to place it on you

So here I am
bleeding myself dry
just so you can sleep at night

A poem composed entirely of lies
(after Amy Kay)

You were never here, not even once. This house isn't haunted because nothing ever died here. You never picked me up. You never even asked to. You never drove me home, taking the long way every time. You overstayed your welcome. I didn't. You loved every girl that came before me. You loved every single one of them, except me.

You never kissed me like you had something to prove. I never had anything to prove. I never looked in the mirror and tried desperately to place the face of the girl staring back at me. The signs were all there, and I didn't miss any of them. Because I knew you just as well as you knew me. I never needed more.

I couldn't have loved you for even one more day. In fact, I never loved you at all. And when he kisses me in his car, I don't think about your hands. Not even once. Not even twice. But it doesn't mean anything. It's not like I still get dizzy every time I pass a white Accord.

When I found out about her, I wasn't angry with you.
I wasn't furious. I wasn't livid.

Just know, I don't have a single regret.
Just know, you were a bad liar. The worst.

Prey

When heartbreak felt like a predator
I curled up in its jaws
and called it a day well spent

I STOOD AT BAGGAGE CLAIM & MISSED YOU SO BAD I HAD TO WRING OUT MY HEART BECAUSE IT WAS SOPPING & SOAPY WITH WANT

Tender
(after Megan Balents)

All because you got in the backseat of that car / Because I liked your taste in music / Because you looked at me like that / like I was the only person in the room / Because every movie we watched / was interrupted by wanting / Because I was used to you / Because I was used to my heart in your mouth / Because I trusted you wouldn't bite down / Because you watched me get dressed in the morning / Because I always caught you staring at me in the mirror / and our eyes bounced off of each other / like we were shy / or something / like we were in love / or something / Because we were always late to the party / Because I didn't care about being late to the party / Because we stood in the doorway / of that hole-in-the-wall joint / and you kissed my lips till they weren't freezing / Because we slept with all the windows open / Because every bed felt miles too big / when I had you next to me / Because I stood at baggage claim / and missed you so bad I had to wring out my heart / because it was sopping and soapy / with want / Because you kept knocking till I opened the door / then kissed me before I could say a word / Because all of my secrets were safe with you / until they weren't / Because I don't miss you anymore / Because that's all your fault / Because it's mine too / Because neither of us are sorry / Because every time I say your name / it sounds like a dirty word / Because I can't keep washing my mouth out with soap / Because I don't think I'll ever hear your voice again / and that kills me a little / But mostly because / after all this time / it finally feels / finished

One for the money, two for the show

I never told you but I loved that orange couch in your old house. I hate admitting it but I still get emotional when I think about the nights we spent lying across it. All the feverish firsts.

One a.m. after that party, and I gave you all my secrets. All my wildest trust. And spent the next hour holding my tongue while you talked about wanting to get out of this town. Tried not to take it personally. Because I knew you needed it like I needed you.

I guess I always knew where this was headed. Ignored the warning signs, all the premonitions. Because you told me you meant it. And I held onto that so tight my knuckles turned white.

If I'm being honest, the lines were blurred but I still read between them. If I'm being honest, I swallowed every word you fed to me.

Even in your sleep you were pulling me closer,
letting me down further.

Despite it all, I would've put money on you and me. Made a foolish bet. Because every time I made you laugh it felt like a gamble. Like the week after your eighteenth birthday, standing on a San Francisco street corner, scratching lottery tickets with dimes and fingernails. Laughter in our chests when we lost. Sometimes it's easy to forget the losing. Just as easy to forget the winning. 100 dollars, splitting me right down the middle. Two months before you lost me.

Mythic

It took me longer than it should have
to pry my fingers from the myth of you and me

Confessions

I never say your name out loud anymore
but sometimes I still search for proof
of your existence

I'm still sweeping for fingerprints
evidence that you ever touched me

There's two-way glass and a videotape
They're asking if I was there
and I can't lie
Lord knows I've tried

I'm not sorry anymore
and I know you never were
but if I take the blame
would it still be the same?

Maybe I don't want to know
how this thing ends

i wish we could've made all of this
worth something

but maybe it's better
we never got to see it through

everything i miss, no longer exists

Walter Mitty

You used to tell me I was perfect
and it was the worst thing you ever said to me

The rot

I'm sorry I eulogized all of the ugly. I'm sorry I took these moments and turned them inside out. Showed the world every mistake you ever made.

Those moments were yours, too. Just as much as they were mine.

I'm sorry I let the cavities have the floor.
The only language they know is decay.

Love wasn't enough.
Even when I wanted it to be. Even when I needed it to be.

There was distance, and avoidance, and then there was you.
Standing in the middle of it all with your hands up. Blameless.

And love wasn't enough to make up for all of those rotten things. And I'm sorry for that. Not because it's my fault. But because one of us has to apologize.

And we both know it won't be you.

Gravedigger

I'm a terrible thing
for burying everything
just to dig it back up again.
Not because it's still alive,
but because I don't want to run out of eulogies to give.

Stranger syndrome

Yesterday I wanted to call and tell you that a stranger in a passing car reminded me of you. And reminded me of that night, last November, when you called just to tell me that you missed me so much, people were starting to look like me.

This isn't to say I miss you. To be candid, sometimes I wish I still did. When I was heartsick, at least I knew the antidote. Now I'm sick with something else altogether.

Because when I try to imagine you it's nearly impossible. And if we spoke now, I know it would be on a bed of eggshells. Stilted conversation saturated in unfamiliarity. And I can't stomach small talk. Not with you. I know you'd tell me you're doing just fine and I'd say the same.

And neither of us would tell the truth. About how you weren't the one for me, even when I wanted you to be. About how I was never going to live up to the version of myself you made up in your mind. About how I know this is for the better. About how that doesn't mean it doesn't still hurt sometimes. Like a broken bone that is long healed.

It still aches when it rains.

Just kids killing time

We were so young. Tucked inside hotel rooms, under covers. Your youth like warm breath on a cold windowpane. Mine like the finger drawing dirty pictures in the steam. But we played grown-ups when we took the train. You always let me have the first free seat. And you woke me up when I fell asleep.

Walking home in the dark was easier with you. With you, the spaces between streetlights felt shorter. With you, I let myself be led

past that old vinegar factory in some miserable part of Illinois neither of us knew. Split my sides in the pouring rain, swore I'd never been more in love with you.

Every part of you was warm and familiar and mine. And maybe sometimes I mistook comfort for intimacy. But when I'm tired like this, all I can remember is that you always touched me with steady hands. And I loved you like we were going steady.

Truthfully, whatever unraveled us can probably be attributed to youth and naivety. But I want you to know you were never just a waiting room for me. You were never a bus stop or a train station or a rest stop along the way. You were my landing place.

When I touch down on the tarmac, just know I'll be thinking of you.

You're the catalyst

So maybe I'm a masochist
because even after all this time
I don't ever want to find someone new to miss

Not a poet, just a liar

The past has become a film that is slightly out of focus. It has receded into something that I can hardly claim. Now, when I think about you, I have to question whether it's unaffected by all the times I slipped into reverie, ghostwrote you and me.

My hands are always cold
and the memory of you warming them up
still reverberates through me
every time I drive past that old movie theater.
But was it my breath or yours that grazed my knuckles that
December afternoon?
Did you hold my hand as we walked into the sun
or did I go it alone?

This thing in my chest is rusting from disuse.
I have never told the truth
when it comes to you.

Tell me something

All the lights turned off as we laid in bed, curled into each other like a set of parentheses. It was my last night with you, my last night in that city until you'd let me back in. We were in the dark when I asked you to tell me something you never had before.

I was always aching for more, even if you had nothing left to give. I wanted to know you like you knew me. I wanted to be as close as you'd let me. I wanted to crawl under your skin.

You told me something, and I swore then that I couldn't love you any more than I did in that darkness. But I did. I always loved you more the next day.

I wrestle with it sometimes, the way I loved you. The way I let you love me. I go over every word you ever said to me. Like they're evidence. Like I'm a crime scene. Like your fingerprints are still all over me.

You ripped me open with the sweetest cruelty.

For the longest time, I couldn't admit my part in the way we fell apart. My part: I couldn't admit that we were.

But the truth is (and always will be), I would've rather had you 1,800 miles away than anyone else up close. And there's something to be said for all the odds that were stacked against us and how much we loved each other in spite of them. But sometimes I think you used the distance between us as an excuse not to love me better.

All the lights turned off as we laid in bed, curled away from each other. It was my last night with you, in the place where it all began. I didn't know it then, but I do now. I was in the dark when I found your silence. You had nothing left to give.

I told you goodnight,
and the power went out.

i guess i'm trying to say i'm sorry for all the times
i hung up the phone with my heart between my teeth

i'm sorry for all the times i kept my mouth shut

we both deserved a lot better than that

belief comes slower / afraid of losing something familiar / till you unfurl your fists / till you stop splitting the thread / till you watch it recede into the faintest ache

Alternate endings
(after Clara McGowan)

You tell me how you feel. It doesn't kill you. It doesn't kill me, either.

Or

You stand there, lit under a streetlamp at 1 a.m., while I sit on the curb. You spell it out for me. You don't miss a single letter. But you miss the point entirely. I don't need you to fix my fuckups. I just need you to hold my hand while I fix them myself.

Or

I say, "Fuck you." I tell you, "I wish someone had told me how this would end. I wouldn't have even started it." But I don't mean any of it. Because the truth of the matter is, regardless of the ending, I wouldn't trade anything for that moment in that shitty bodega when you looked at me like I was the most beautiful thing you'd ever seen. My hair frizzy and my skin sallow. I wouldn't trade anything for how it felt, standing still with you. Like I wasn't late for anything. Like I was right on time.

Or

Your laughter in my mouth is more holy than any silly little poem I could ever write.

Or

You leave. It doesn't kill me. It doesn't kill you, either. Your laughter in my mouth isn't holy. It isn't anything. It's just a ghost that passes through me on my way to work. And I sit with it for as long the traffic light allows me. But then the light turns green. And I keep on driving.

When everything holy was mistaken for a curse

I think about all the time I wasted hating you
when I should have been thanking you.

I mistook angels for ghosts. I mistook guidance for haunting. What I believed to be heartbreak was really blazing freedom in disguise.

Which is to say I'm so fucking grateful
nothing happened the way I wanted it to.

thank god i'm not who i was

thank god for change's sweet release

Magnolia

Though my heart is crazed with cracks,
I wouldn't erase a single one.

This isn't a love story except it is

It's January. And I've been wondering where I've been.

It's February. And I cry lonesome on the phone. If this is what love has made you, please tell me how to absolve myself. But then you're here. Or I'm there. With your heartbeat pressed against mine, who can tell the difference?

It's March. And you come home because the world is ending in more ways than one. You hold me tightly. And I tell you that it's hard to remember that this isn't the end. You don't correct me.

It's April. And I fool myself. Over and over again. Which is to say this silence is swollen, even when I pretend it's not. I walk around with shards of my heart in my mouth. And I smile bloody when my mother asks how I'm holding up.

It's May. And I'm considering ripping my heart out but I'm not sure when the warranty expires.

It's June. And I look into his eyes and tell myself I'm not looking for a glimpse of you in them. I lose track of the number of white lies I tell him. When he asks me what I did for my birthday, I think of you inside me.

It's July. And you're playing the drums somewhere and I'm writing somewhere else and the fact that those two things will never exist in the same room again doesn't hurt like it used to. The universe is expanding. I hope it's being kind to you, too.

It's August. And I'm not wondering where I've been. I'm right here.

January, after dark

I want to ask you the worst thing you've ever done.
I want to ask if it's me.

Close the door, you're letting all the cold air in

What would have happened if we'd left it alone? If we'd walked away without turning back? Sometimes I think you are a door I should've kept closed. Should've locked and thrown away the key. Should've smashed the key. Should've smashed the whole goddamn door.

But then I remember that night in October, the way I would've stayed up all night, just to get it right. I remember the blame that we passed between us like a dirty secret. I remember how I mistook that for love. I remember just how many things I mistook for love. And I remember that the safest I ever felt in my whole entire life was in your darkness. And how that makes me unspeakably sad for the person I used to be.

But the truth of the matter is, I could have closed every door. Turned every lock. And it wouldn't have made a damn bit of a difference. You knew just as well as I did that if you knocked, I would have broken any lock. Just to hear you say my name.

Just to try again.

Broken lock

He looks down at me, his eyes dark. The orange light cast from outside my apartment creates sharp shadows that cut across his face. Chills run down the backs of my legs as nostalgia settles under my skin. But I've spent the past month preceding this night reminding myself not to equate familiarity with safety. That's not a mistake I'm willing to make twice.

So far, we've been painfully polite with each other. Asking broad and courteous questions, careful to dance around the elephant in the room. God forbid we step on each other's toes. God forbid one of us might *hurt* the other.

We're being so well-mannered, it's nauseating.

A pocket of silence forms between us, and I can sense the elephant planning its exit strategy. Subtly, he shifts his body closer, so that we're scarcely touching. The little hairs on the back of my neck prickle to attention. Reminiscence lingers on the base of my tongue. I do my best to ignore it, rationalizing it as a bodily reaction.

"What I did to you . . ." he starts, and I let out a sigh.

He cuts himself off at my reaction, a question forming in his expression.

I blink. His face still looks half-apparition. Part of me can't believe he's actually here, sitting in front of me on my newly purchased green couch, trying to give me some sort of belated closure.

"I don't really want to talk about it." I try to keep my voice light, indifferent. "We've moved on, haven't we?"

He studies my face. My eyes, my nose, my mouth. Like he's trying to commit me to memory. He shakes his head.

I look away. It was a question I already knew the answer to, but the answer itself is still unnerving. I try to regain my balance, tilting my head. "So, you missed me?" My tone is teasing.

He says my name, quietly. It goes through me like a needle. Like heaven threaded with hell. I'd tucked away any hope of ever hearing him say it again.

The smile drops from my face.

He moves even closer, until I can feel the flush of his skin against my own. Until I can feel his breath against my cheek. I look away, but a thin, buzzing energy begins to bloom across my skin like films of lace.

It's as if I haven't progressed a single step. We might as well be in my bedroom back home. White walls, books stacked against them. Clothes strewn across the floor.

I risk a glance at his face and find his mouth twisted into a grimace. "Please, just let me say I'm sorry—" I cut him off, shaking my head. It seems foolish to accept something so obvious, so long overdue. It feels closer to pity than I'm comfortable with. And the asking price of my dignity is far greater than a mislaid apology.

Neither of us says anything. After a minute I sigh, my gaze and demeanor relenting. He senses it. We offer each other reluctant smiles.

He reaches up as if he wants to touch my face but thinks better of it. "You know, I barely recognized you." The air crackles between us. "You're different."

My spine straightens. He isn't wrong. I've also never felt more like myself.

He stares at me. I stare back. It passes between us, a glimmer of everything simmering beneath the surface. Gone is the pretense of stilted civility. I am now acutely aware of how alone we are. And how late it is.

"You know what I keep thinking about?"

He catches me off guard. I can feel my features rearranging themselves. I try my best not to look curious.

"We were here, in Chicago, back in September. And we were sitting in the courtyard of your hotel, outside the pool." His expression slides into nostalgia, tangled with something else I can't decipher.

"And you were sitting in between my legs. It was so quiet."

I roll my eyes at his sentimentality, but I can feel my face get warm. "Right, well, we were always good at that. The quiet thing." I'm aiming for sardonic, but my voice comes out thin.

I glance around the room quickly, trying to get a breath in. I'm still trying to decide if this night is something I'm going to regret. I tuck my hair behind my ear, then untuck it. I can't sit still.

Steeling myself, I fix my gaze somewhere over his shoulder, a small pinprick of light across the river. "You knew that I loved you." I try to say it clinically, factually. I shift my eyes to his, impassive. "And it wasn't small. None of it was."

He looks across the couch at me, dazed. My heart stutters. I let the silence stretch out until it goes taut.

"You knew I did, too." His voice is hoarse.

"Did I?"

He hesitates, then pushes onward, "Before you—I mean, nothing else was even real."

I exhale, then nod, slowly, in restrained agreement.

He holds my gaze. This time he doesn't stop himself. He reaches up and brushes my hair back from my face. I fight the urge to hold his hand there.

"I don't anymore, you know," I say, mostly to myself. My voice scratches against my throat.

"I know."

Slowly, he leans in closer, searching my eyes for permission. My head swims. I lose focus, trying to count the number of times we've ended things. Only to find ourselves right back at the start. Was there ever any other recourse?

His lips brush my own. A position so tenderly familiar and shockingly foreign that it's staggering.

"What you did to me . . ."

He exhales softly into my mouth. "I know." He says it like an apology. This, I'll accept.

I'm well aware that I've lost my footing. A million questions crowd my throat.

"What if—"

He shakes his head. He knows me, my inability to let problems go unresolved.

His fingertips feel cold brushing my cheek. It would take less than an inch to close the space between our mouths, but he takes his time.

In this space, I rifle through moments, through memories. But there's no time. There's only time for this.

When I feel his mouth, sweet and desperate, touch my own, it's different than how I remember it. It's like kissing someone else entirely.

But somehow, I can let this problem go unresolved. Somehow, this isn't a problem at all.

Hindsight

It's easier to write about what I see in the rearview mirror
than anything that I'm crashing into headfirst

Contaminated

Your name in my unmade bed / and I'm still scrubbing the sheets / But something about your delicate deceit / makes it so hard to leave / Your mouth / and the truth / and all the space in between / Something about the way / you're looking at me / And I'm trying to fight it / trying to practice what I preach / But it's been two weeks / and I'm still sighing your name before I sleep

Firebird

There's a fire in the backseat but we don't notice. Your hands skate across my skin and all of my nerve endings fray.

Your touch like blue smoke. Your scent like uncut wood.

I try to rationalize this and miss all the warning signs while doing so.

Your thumbs press into my pulse points and I feel close to the sky. It's balmy and blue.

Come back to me, you say.

I always do, don't I?

You touch me in places I never thought I could be unraveled by. The insides of my wrists, the backs of my knees, in between my shoulder blades.

You come away stained. So do I.

The smoke thickens and

god, I hope I always remember us like this. Fevered and undone. A fire burning in the backseat that neither of us notice, much less put out.

Time machine

Maybe one day I'll write about how this all makes sense, in the grand scheme of things: you walking me home beneath a promising sky. Or maybe I won't and it doesn't.

Either way, I want you to know

you were never just something to cut my teeth on. Sure, we were young. Sure, we were foolish. But you were never just a milestone or a checkpoint to pass. And seeing you again doesn't feel like walking backwards. It doesn't feel like retracing my steps. You used to make time stop. Now you smile at me and everything just keeps moving forward.

For keeps

In the end
you forgive my messes
and I forgive yours

2.0

It's different this time
I know you feel it too
It's softer
but it's easier to hold onto

41°56'N 87°39'15"W

Your lips against my open palm
and I want to tell you that it's okay
if we don't know the final destination.
The map was thrown out ages ago.
There are a million routes to take
and I don't care where they lead.
As long as you're next to me.

What's in a name

I love the way
you say my name.
You don't say it often,
but when you do
it makes my heart skip,
makes my head turn.
Once,
you said it so tenderly
I swore every person
that had ever said my name
had been saying it wrong.
Because the way it tripped off your tongue,
the way it tumbled past your lips,
was nothing but
right,
right,

right.

Love poem #44

So you're standing there, looking a little like you love me. And I'd like to say it doesn't scare me but baby, I'm out of practice writing love poems. For so long it was about the leaving and the losing and the longing. And now it's about the way you make my coffee just right. The way your mouth tastes like mine. It's about your hands in my curls, your mouth open on my throat. It's about Friday night in the emergency room, your grip on the back of my chair. It's about how you came back and covered more ground in a single look than anyone else could in ten months. And, if nothing else, it's about how nothing has ever made more sense to me than your toothbrush on my sink.

It's about the way we're trying our best to get it right. About how even if we don't, I'll spend my whole life being glad we tried.

A ♥ We're trying our best to get it right

& even if we don't, i'll spend my whole life being glad we tried

Love languages

Telling me I'm right / Reading my poems / Re-reading my poems / Letting the dog out / Letting me in / Kissing my forehead / in a crowd full of people / Love letters / Comfortable silence / Offering to drive / Flowers in the middle of the week / Sheltering my strength / just as much as my softness / Making me laugh / Holding me tight / Kissing my fingers / Kissing my fuckups / Knowing looks / across a crowded room / and loving me / when I'm not looking / Showing me all your favorite songs / because baby / I want the whole damn catalogue / Our own secret club / now that we're in love / Letting me fall apart / and not faulting me for it / And loving my fault lines / just as much / as all of the unbroken land in between / Giving me space / Pulling me close / You ask me what I dreamt about / before you even open your eyes / and you mean it / You tell me you love me / and you really / really / mean it

References

Love is a smoke alarm [1] Love is a big stretch [2] Love is your mouth to my ear [3] Love is your eye to the viewfinder [4] Love is a really long guitar solo [5] Love is the street slick with rain [6] Love is barefoot in the grass after a party [7] Love is fizzy brains [8] Love is the song I played in your car [9] Love is the golden slant of light on the train [10] Love is kissing my teeth [11] Love is knocking down my door [12] Love is come here on a street corner [13] Love is a grocery list [14] Love is thick socks on the kitchen floor [15] Love is hands on the table [16] Love is a matchbox unstruck [17] Love is early [18] Love is blue hour mornings [19] Love is your heart rising before the alarm [20] Love is under the sheets, flash-lit whispers [21] Love is the current [22] Love is a swell [23] Love is mouths wide, spills of laughter [24] Love is you know what I mean? Love is yeah, I know what you mean [25] [26]

Dog-ear

A minute left before the song fades away.
I love you so I say it.
No holds barred,
not anymore.

Baby, I'd recognize your love anywhere.
In another town, another state.

I'm glad we stayed up late.
We sit on the porch till our weariness calls us in.
I dog-ear these moments
so I don't lose my place.
I want to come back to them when this all goes to hell.

We laugh so deep it hurts our ribs.
We tell ourselves we're the exception—
the sequel that's better than the original.
You squeeze my hand so tight I almost believe it.

Our bones are lazy but we don't fault them for it.
We watch *It's Always Sunny in Philadelphia*
and you blow smoke into my mouth.
In the morning, you wake me up to watch the sunrise.
We walk half a mile in the rain just to stare at a bruised sky.

Writing on the wall

Looking back, I guess there were warning signs.
It's funny, how anything can look like an omen
when held up against the right light.

Broken clocks

The night split us down the middle. Whether fated or the result of some indecent act of cruelty, it fractured us in a vague, yet irretrievable way.

A photo, taken just moments before a disaster. The entire night, the entire party, could have been that photo—taken with slow shutter speed, one blissfully ignorant moment bleeding into the next. The dinner we ate on his back porch, low sun casting the back alley into golden glow. The first few drinks, my body buzzing. The people, the music, all of it was perfect. And I was perfectly unwitting. I'd never loved him more.

And then, like a fist to glass, came the crack in the clock.

I'd been waiting in line for the bathroom when she came up to me, placing her hand on my forearm like we were old friends. Bleary-eyed, I leaned in, trying to hear her over the speakers. She slurred into my ear, and my skin started to prickle coldly. Like I'd accidentally flipped to the wrong channel—a subdermal static I couldn't turn off.

"I don't understand," I kept saying. But I did.

I tried to focus on breathing, letting the seconds unwind slowly. Like a stopwatch counting down to something I had been given no time to brace myself for.

The party was still happening all around me, scratching at the edges of my consciousness, but in the kitchen everything was balanced on a razor's edge. All the clocks in the room had stopped cold. It felt like cruel proof.

We've always had a shelf life.

He was standing across the kitchen, still laughing into his beer, while I called time of death at 1:16 a.m.

Worst of all, I think a piece of me always knew it was going to come down to this. Down to the minute, down to the wire.

Down to the exact second we broke.

Paradise

I wake up and I'm not sure what I'm holding onto anymore. All I know is that my hands are bloody. This used to be paradise. This kitchen, this back porch. Dancing through summer nights. Jazz on vinyl. Something burning in the kitchen, something burning in the space between our chests. Now I smoke just to remember how your mouth tastes. Like ash and bad luck. Now I wake up and my hands unfurl and all my questions stain the sheets. This used to be paradise. Now I wake up and something is burning and all I can do is watch it go up in smoke.

If people are puzzle pieces

I am still yours more than any other's.
That has to count for something.

Slow dance

It roared in my chest,
something vicious and unforgiving.
You cupped my face in your hands
and I thought only of my pores.
While I tried to drown out the animal
locked in my ribcage.
The one with the voice like a siren.
The temperature rose.
The song sustained.

And you looked at me
like I was something you could touch.
But you couldn't.
You never could.

WHEN YOU HELD ME
DID I FEEL WHOLE?

Simple is a dirty word

If I could pluck one moment from that first summer, a singular instant that stands apart from the rest of those fleeting seconds in the sun, it would be this: me and you under a tunnel of trees, our wheels turning quickly down the street near the beach. Careless, and free.

In my mind I knew that everything, including that moment, including us, had an expiration date. But I wanted to pause time, right when the sun broke through the leaves, casting strange and beautiful shadows over our faces. I wanted to stop all the clocks from running forward.

Everything I loved about you exists inside that moment. Before you left me stained with longing, turned me into a stranger. Before we buried all of our doubts and sorrows in a shallow grave and gave this one more shot. Before that party. Before you told me in the dark that I was all that mattered, and I pretended that I was already asleep.

In the pools of sunlight my tires were splashing through, amidst the leaves, driving too fast with my hair swept up by the wind, everything was simple.

You weren't loving me until you were blue in the face. You weren't holding onto me so tight that I crumbled in your fists. It wasn't winter, it wasn't snowing. I wasn't falling apart. It was summer, it was scorching. I was with you.

And it was simple.

~~Peace~~ and quiet

Silence is a language we've become fluent in
and all I can hear is the water
dripping from the faucet
getting stuck in my ears
And I keep shaking my head
upside down
trying to get the future we once imagined
out of my mind

The cinema played a foreign film tonight
and I thought that maybe
another language
could soften the words stuck in our throats
But we walked home,
hands loosely tangled together
silence filling the space between our fingers
Because the only words we have left to speak
are the ones we leave unsaid
And now
we're sitting across from each other
feeling the end beat down upon us with closed fists
Long ago
we made time to the beat of our hearts
but now
the stillness in our chests is resounding

and you forgot to turn off the tap

Halfway gone

You touch me and I skid away
from the foreign act of tenderness.
I pour salt in the wound just to feel
a different kind of pain.

Out-of-body

You stand on the street and try to pull yourself together. You're so tired your hands hurt. You're having trouble falling asleep these days. In all your dreams, your punches never land.

You fall in love with him again. And you could've sworn it meant something, him coming back the way he did. But maybe all it means is that he came back, strung out and unchanged. He asks if you believe him when he says he can be better.

You cover your mouth with your hand. Quiet yourself. Everything goes right before it goes wrong.

You get Sick. Your life goes missing. In this blank space, it's too dark to see your own hand in front of your face. You are standing at the edge of something, arms outstretched. But you can't reach yourself.

You are out of your body.

You sit on the porch with a boy. False spring and all of that. You play gin rummy and you are viscerally aware of how much he loves you. You wonder what he could possibly say to make you forget about what he did in that goddamn kitchen.

You're on a losing streak.

You think you'll be better by October. You're wrong.

Unspinning my spine

There are lyrics that tell me to remember that I have a body. I tell them that I have never forgotten. I have memorized every curve in my figure like bends in a river. Yet when I trace them with fingers and nails, I find myself cast adrift, time and time again.

These silver bones in my wrist, this heart like a crimson animal, I have known it all. Known it like a weapon. Known it like a knife.

They tell me to remember that I have a body.
I tell them I wish I could forget.

See you soon

I call my mother crying
and she tells me I'm just in the thick of it.
It'll look different when it all settles down.

Over the phone, she tells me
there's a new beginning
in the crease between moments.
Over the phone, she tells me
there's no wrong time
to start over.
I call my mother crying
and she lends me her breath
until I've caught mine.

Before we hang up,
I say,
See you soon.
But what I really mean is,
I'm never lonely knowing you're in the world with me.

Elegy

Most of all
I am grieving myself

Cutting you out with a dull knife

I have grown accustomed to the worst parts of you.

You are like
a cold hand on the back of my neck.
You are like
an ache in my molar.

I write about leaving
but most times I can't finish the poem.
Most times
I can't even finish the sentence.

How much should I have to endure for the sake of your good intentions?

THIS HOUSE ISN'T HAUNTED, BUT THE WALLS STILL SPEAK. THIS HOUSE ISN'T HAUNTED, BUT THE TENANT MIGHT BE.

Cloudy with a chance of misery

I keep thinking it'll get better / and when it doesn't / I blame the weather / But the clouds crowding the sky / have nothing to do / with the art of getting by / So I guess my mind's the only thing I have to blame / All the movies I watch end the same / with the sun setting / over a happy ending / and the credits roll by / and I try to feel fine / but I come up empty-handed / Nothing's going how I planned it

This house isn't haunted / but the walls still speak / This house isn't haunted / but the tenant might be / Because as much as I try / nothing seems to change / I keep checking the weather / but I still end up getting caught in the rain

Blue

Fell asleep under static light / Kissed you messy when I woke up / Funny, how we thought we had it all figured out / Held me in bed, late afternoon / Couldn't tell because of your windowless room / Loved you / More-than-loved you / Only showered once together that winter / Learned to pull away just to get you up close / All that static, hissing under my skin / Don't remember it getting dark, just that it did / Just that, when we woke up, I kissed you just to make sure I was still there

Guts for garters

I'm sick with resentment. There are so many words I've swallowed, just to keep my anger at bay. But now they're coming up, sitting in my throat like bile.

My heart catches fire as I drive down Lakeshore. My throat burns as I walk through your back door. I sit at your kitchen table like my body isn't a burning building.

I tell my therapist I saw a little girl thrashing around in the supermarket and her mother was seeing red. I saw myself, doubled.

When I am angry I am both the punisher
and the one being punished.

I tell my therapist I have too much anger and not enough body.

She tells me I don't seem angry. I just seem sad.
I tell her I don't know how to tell the difference.

They both feel like being burned at the stake.

Stillwater

The pain ripples from the inside out. Like you skipped a goddamn stone across my heart. Before it all began, I believe I told you that I would gladly endure this pain. That I would welcome it if it meant getting to hold you, for even a minute. That I would thank you for letting me fall in love with you. Even if it hurt all the way down.

You asked me this morning if I would take it back. If I would've liked to know a world without the scar on your hand, without the green in your eyes. If I would've liked to know a world where love doesn't end with all the stones at the bottom of the pond. Where the water is still, like glass. Where nothing hurts, but I never get the chance to love you.

Mistake

He bends down to pick up his backpack and, once again, I'm overwhelmed with the urge to pull myself back into the present. To not think about what came before this, or what comes after. To not compare this to the first time we said goodbye, when he knelt to tie his shoes and I pressed the heels of my hands to my eyes and gasped for breath.

I'm consumed, trying to commit this all to memory. The way he looks. The way he feels when I tug his shirt and pull him into me one last time. The way his neck smells as I bury my face into it.

"I still—" He inhales sharply. "I love you."

I hesitate. Then a swell of tenderness rises, swallowing up any scraps of pride I might've been holding onto. I whisper it back, my voice threadbare.

This doesn't stitch any wounds together the way I wish it would. My throat is dry and twisted. I feel like there's something I'm supposed to say but I can't find the words.

"I think you're making a mistake," he says.

A pang slices through me. And I feel a wash of longing—not for him, but for last year, the year before. For the people we were before we knew the ache of leaving, the ache of being left.

I don't tell him this, but if this is a mistake, it doesn't feel like it. Even as he pulls away from me and takes a step back, then another. If this is a mistake, it feels nowhere near it. It feels closer to inevitable.

Even as he presses his lips to my forehead. Even as he leans his temple against mine and pleads with me one last time.

I shake my head. He walks away.

If this is a mistake, it's mine to make.

Just not in this one

In another life
I swallowed every doubt
and instead
offered you a mouthful
of forgiveness

So this is it (again)

I shut the door. But if I'm not yours I don't know whose I am anymore. Were you listening when I said that I loved you? I know it's not the way you want it, but you have to believe me when I say if I had the choice I wouldn't be walking away.

God, I wish this turned out better.

It's hard to breathe when I think about that night in the kitchen when, for the first time, I couldn't bear for you to touch me. When I think about the fight in the stairwell, the train ride home that I can scarcely recall.

This isn't how we planned it. And sometimes my mind still clings to late afternoon in your bed, how I held your face between my palms. Sometimes it stings to remember how desperately I loved you.

I don't think there's anything poetic about the way this all worked out. But here we are, standing in the doorway again. Just like that night in January. Between hallway and home. Between strangers and natives.

I fist your T-shirt in my hand before you go. I'm still coming to terms with all the ways we've broken this. Must be some kind of record.

I shut the door. And just like that, you're not mine anymore.

Last call

So I'll go home and sleep it off
And my head pounds with dreams of us

It barely hurts
I'm used to worse

You know I wouldn't tell you
even if it did

On not writing

I'm restless.
Whenever I'm doing something
I am sure that I'm supposed to be doing something else.

Haven't I said all that I've needed to say?
Isn't everything I write an echo of my own suffering?

The price of departure

Every time I see you
I know you
less and less

There is nothing stranger
than watching you
become a stranger

Rimshot (ba-dum tss)

I end up next to the drum set at a gig and spend the opening act trying to ignore the implication. Is it still a coincidence if I assign meaning to it? The bass burns through my belly and I think of you, just five miles south. Sticks in your hands and your foot on the pedal. You're keeping time and I'm keeping up appearances. Laughing at jokes and trying to remind myself I exist. The drummer winks and hands me the set list. Our hands touch and it feels like a punchline. Different boy, same rimshot. We all know how the joke goes. The drummer and a girl walk into a bar. No one makes it out unscathed.

OF ALL OF THE THINGS THAT CANNOT BE UNDONE, YOU & I ARE MY FAVORITE ONE

Serrated

I don't know where the edges of this are
but I know they're jagged
Which is to say
I've never been good at clean breaks

While we're here

Come over tonight / I'll do my best impression of who I used to be / I'll crystallize / with your eyes on me / It isn't right / but it's a relief / To pretend I'm not so weak / You'll unravel our future while I sit idly by / When I don't love you back / I'm the prettiest vision you've ever seen

Come over / we'll lie across the bed / We'll reminisce / and it's unhealthy at best / We'll mourn the inside jokes we had to retire / now the only one left is what we've done to each other

Come over / I'll coax you through your lovesick spells / I'll let you hold me / if just for a while / You'll kiss up my spine / You'll hold my hand to your heart / And it would all be so endearing / if not for my misgivings I can't seem to give up

Come over / and I'll kiss you / I won't feel a thing / I'll kiss you / and you'll tell me nothing's missing

And maybe you're right / At least it won't hurt

In the end / it's just a stale joke

Com-pul-sive

I look up the definition of compulsive
and call it inconclusive
But I'm cutting ties
just to knot them back together
god
nothing about this is tender

I draw a line
just to cross it
I wish someone had told me
when you fall apart
it's not all at once
but bit by bit

Older

You will grow up and look just like you,
but with wrinkles around your eyes when you smile.
With laugh lines you'll get from someone else.
You will look staggeringly different,
but achingly the same.
And because of the choices we both have made,
I won't be a witness to any of it.

Winter

I'm sorry I loved like I was lingering in the doorway.
Loving you hurt. Not loving you hurt.
I didn't know which way to turn.

Okay

It's okay, I guess. You'll meet some girl in art school. With dyed hair and a nose ring and she'll be lovely and detached and drive you up the wall. And it's okay. Really, it is. You'll tell her things you told me once. In reverent tones, with your body covering hers. She'll love something that I hated and at first it's jarring but then it's normal. Refreshing, even. Which is to say loving someone that's not me is strange until it's not. Her laugh is husky and she is blunt and she is not meticulous but she is careful with the things that matter. You are the thing that matters. And you'll show up at her door and she'll say something that makes you roll your eyes with affection and all of a sudden loving me seems like something you did in another life. And it's okay, I guess. It has to be. And maybe I'll cross your mind once a month or so, on your walk home. And you'll wonder what I'm doing, and who I'm doing it with. And you'll realize that it was always supposed to happen this way. And it won't kill you like it used to. Not even a little bit. Not even close.

Dearly departed

I don't think it's any big secret
that I was too busy collapsing in on myself
to love you
the way I wanted to

Flannels on the floor

I wish I knew what I was waiting for.

The drive home is strained and I'm sorting through my feelings, trying to find the one that fits. The one that has a name. I miss you but not in the way you want me to. I miss you like I miss your laugh and the way you say *goddamn*. You miss me like you miss the way I looked at you on the train. The way my tongue curls around your name.

You ask me on the elevator if I think we're just too young for something like this. And I blame it on our timing while I fumble with the keys. Which you take to mean the same thing. But what I really mean is that we each loved the other at different times. And I can't tell you how much that kills me. So I keep quiet. I squeeze your hand. And we keep missing each other. In more ways than one.

The only real thing

I thought things would be different now
that itself is something to mourn

Lapse

I know I took it back whenever I wanted / I know you felt like you never really lost it / I never stopped calling / even after I left / Knew you'd come running / and I couldn't stomach what was next

You said give it time / I got bored out of my mind / Come down / let me take you apart / like you're still mine

Can we please pretend I left sooner / Didn't call you last September / All those times you leaned in close / and I laughed it off / Said I loved you / when I really meant your ghost

And it was selfish / God, I know / Holding on when you wouldn't let go / Told myself I was always honest / but wasn't I the one who called it? / All those times I walked out / just to walk back in / Never thought you'd wait up for me / Never thought you wouldn't say when

i know you're defensive
i know you resent me
you know i had to
leave like that

just so i couldn't come back

Living it up / you can have it all

So there you go again / faking empathy / and splitting hairs / over who twisted the knife first / who twisted it deeper / Baby between you and me / I think we both know the answer

Pacify you over something you did / Stick your tongue down her throat / then cry on my shoulder / And I wasn't tired enough to give it a rest / I was slow to start / and slow to finish / and you were there the whole time / *you were there the whole time*

Baby what was I doing / while you were touching her? / Baby what am I supposed to do / with a counterfeit history? / How do I paint over false memories / erase distorted footage / Baby how many times will you ruin what you're given?

So there you go again / faking remorse / and kicking stones / so I feel like the cruel one / You had it all planned out / A house in the hills / covered in fake plants / that look a lot like the real thing / I'm a clueless housewife and you get to fuck around

I hope you get everything you've ever wanted / and I hope I never hear a thing about it

I HOPE YOU GET EVERYTHING YOU'VE EVER WANTED & I HOPE I NEVER HEAR A THING ABOUT IT

Baby be good

Don't you know how to go home alone? / You're just a cheap replica / who doesn't know someone else's hand from his own / Your lack of conviction / is a stunning addiction / The sting of your teeth / the shock of your wake / The waste of my time / my longest mistake / And when you reached for me empty / I thought it was love / It was never as good as I thought it was you're so devout in the way you let me down

Stranger complex

I bet you wish I had a savior complex
I bet you envision me leaving you
in the jaws of something wild

And I bet you think I don't think about you at all

I bet you don't know that the thought of your face
on that June afternoon
still makes my stomach twist

I bet you wish I stayed
and told you to point to where it hurt
I bet you wish I was an open wound
just like you

I bet you wish I had a savior complex
instead of all my other fucking neuroses
that I bet you wish I could just get over

Did you mean it when you said
you felt less alone
when you saw my face?

I bet you wish you did

Slasher

You said once there was always a part of me you couldn't get to, something tender you couldn't touch. Your inflated sense of self, entitled to carve out my insides. Taking and taking and taking.

As if I was ever going to let you have it.
As if I hadn't already given you enough.

Splinter

I couldn't cut you out of me until I had to.
Like a splinter, subdermal.
You suck the blood out of my finger
and act like it isn't your fault I'm bleeding.
And I'm not saying I'm blameless.
In any of it.
I was the one who ran my fingers over split wood.
But I'm so fucking tired of feeling guilty
for walking away
from something that did nothing
but leave me bloody.

how much of the way
you loved me
shaped me into
the person i am?

how much credit do
i owe you?

how much blame?

Heat lightning

They say lightning never strikes twice, and they're right. The second time we loved each other was less of a thunderstorm and more of a quiet crumbling.

You called yourself complex to justify every time you lost your head. Let me be the one to find it for you. And I called it a saga, the way you handed me the blame like it meant something. And maybe it did. Maybe it meant too much.

I held it just long enough to realize it was burning my palms.

When I think back on it, I know that I knew better. I was just pretending I didn't. I knew I shouldn't touch the burning stove. But I kept craving the moment before my skin blistered. When your love was so scathing it felt ice cold.

Cool girl

Does he love you?
Or does he love the person he is when he's with you?

Do you make him feel like the kind of man he'd like to be?

There's an unholy truth in being the funhouse mirror in a relationship. He looks at you and sees how you see him. He curls around his warped reflection at night.

And as your penance, you surrender the kind of love that sees you, that knows you, that accepts you. For your sins and your mess and your flaws. You concede to being relentlessly misunderstood, if it means you get to hold his tired head at the end of the night.

You're a golden girl, a statue on a pedestal, a cool girl, a good wife. You're wearing his boxers. You're holding a mirror.

The plot

I wanted all that pain to be worth something.
I wanted to be able to cash it in.
For good art, or good karma, or a good time.

Couldn't I at least make a story out of it?
Nothing award-winning,
Just something to wring a laugh out of
at dinner parties.

I don't think that's how this works.

I wanted to believe that my life was made up of
beginnings and endings.

I'm beginning to suspect
it's all just one big middle.

Staying Tender for the Promise of Something Better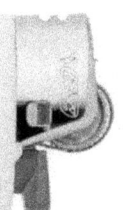

Fever

Sweat gathers between my breasts, a droplet sliding south till it reaches my navel. The sun stains my cheeks. It's been months since I've been this warm.

When it's like this, it's hard to remember any of it actually happened. The emergency room visits in the dead of winter, the watery smiles, the hands scrambling for purchase, for solidity, for anything vaguely resembling hope.

When it's like this, it's easier to think of this year as simply an exercise in loneliness. Rather than the most desolate months of my life.

Despite the heat wave, there's still proof of winter. I wear it in my hips. A warm breeze passes through me, but my pulse thrums beneath my skin, reminding me, under no uncertain terms, that I'm here, alive, sweating.

The winter passed, like it always does.

I'm still trying to figure out how to exist in the aftermath.

Peace

If I give myself peace / If I paint the walls blue / If I fall asleep in the sun / with a book split open on my stomach / If I eat fresh fruit with my hands / If I pour coffee for the one I love / If I run with the dogs / If I put on an album I can feel in my bones / If I trust myself unflinchingly / If I believe my life is meant to be joyful / and soft / and quiet / If I sink into the relief / of letting myself breathe / If I never let myself down / What will become of me / of everything I used to believe

sometimes healing

looks a lot like leaving

Touchstone

You are no longer the reference point
from which I measure everything good in my life

A tuesday in september

I'm not sad about it anymore
but sometimes my chest still pinches
when I think about the way we circled the drain.
About the way you said my name.

And I'm not lonely
so I don't know why I still cry
when I wake up in the middle of the night
and no one is breathing on the nape of my neck.

And I don't know why it wasn't you.
I don't know why you had to be so kind
while I was breaking your heart.
I don't know why you couldn't have been decent
when I loved you and it mattered.

I'm not sad about it anymore
but sometimes it still feels like I'm drowning in
something unknown.

But I know it's getting easier to catch my breath on my own.

On the way home

There is a place where I am loved for none of my accomplishments, for none of my resiliency, for none of my strength despite despite despite. There is a place where I can be foolish at the risk of ugliness, where I can cry at the risk of weakness, where I can fail. Again and again and again. In this place, I am split wide open, sweet and sickly. In this place, I am loved. Not despite, but because.

Better

I'll get better. I'll learn to sleep in the middle of the bed. I'll drink loose leaf tea. I'll get over all the things that have hurt me. I'll be softer, kinder with myself. I'll visit Banff, and Switzerland, and Edinburgh. I'll do all the things I've ever wanted to do. I'll try not to make this about me. I'll be a good daughter, good friend, good lover. I'll buy produce locally. I'll buy flowers and won't wait until they're three weeks dead before I throw them out. I'll learn to leave well enough alone. I'll get better. I'll let someone in. One of these days, I'll let someone see the rotten side of my heart. I'll let them love me anyway.

things are changing & I am, too
I hope it's for the better

I think it's for the better

Come back to back to back

My underwear around my ankles at 1:07 a.m. / In the mirror / the girl looking back at me / is bleary-eyed / with a crooked smile / and looks so familiar / I could cry / I crawl into bed / drunk and happy and alone / It's quiet / and I'm thinking about how I'm always finding myself in the most unlikely places / Thinking about how I've never missed anyone as desperately as I've missed myself / Thinking about tomorrow / how I'll cook dinner in my underwear / then wipe the crumbs from my lips / And think about how maybe / while the old me was leaving / she saved a spot for me here

Notes

The title "Misery is the thing with feathers" references the poem "'Hope' is the thing with feathers" by Emily Dickinson.

"These are the things we don't talk about" was written after Caitlin Conlon's poem of the same title, in her chapbook *Cavity*.

"Linguistics" was written after Caitlin Conlon's poem of the same title, in her collection *The Surrender Theory*.

"A poem composed entirely of lies" was written after Amy Kay's poem of the same title.

"Tender" was written after Megan Balents' poem of the same title.

"Alternate endings" was written after Clara McGowan's poem of the same title, in her collection *This Is All I Have To Give You*.

The title "What is in a name" references a line in *Romeo and Juliet* by William Shakespeare.

The title "Living it up / you can have it all" references a lyric in the song "Nothing Good Ever Happens at the Goddamn Thirsty Crow" by Father John Misty.

"Cool girl" was inspired by and has references to the song "Complex" by Katie Gregson-MacLeod. The title also references *Gone Girl* by Gillian Flynn.

The title "Come back to back to back" references a lyric in the song "Larabar" by Wet.

Acknowledgements

Thank you to my brilliant editor, Caitlin Conlon. This book would be nowhere near where it is today without you.

Thank you to the poets and authors who read this book in all its stages. Thank you to Makenzie Campbell, Ari B. Cofer, Caitlin Conlon, Zane Fredericks, Haley Jakobson, Shelby Leigh, Trista Mateer, and Clara McGowan.

Thank you to Lauren Tepfer. I cannot thank you enough for your gorgeous work on this cover.

Thank you to my mother, whose love and support has undoubtedly made me the person I am today. My favorite person on planet Earth. You're the best (not that I'm biased or anything).

And thank you for reading. I love you. I mean it.

About the author

Audrey Emmett is a writer and visual artist from the San Francisco Bay Area, currently based in Chicago, Illinois. When she's not writing, she's most likely reading, running by the lake, or watching stand-up comedy.

Don't Be a Stranger is her second collection of poetry.

Connect with her on Instagram (@audrey_emmett) and TikTok (@audreyemmett).

www.ingramcontent.com/pod-product-compliance
Lightning Source LLC
Chambersburg PA
CBHW022103090426
42743CB00008B/705